AMBI
SCORECARD

Thanks to the Creative Team:

Kerri Morrison

Hamish MacDonald

Shannon Waller

Jennifer Bhatthal

Christine Nishino

Willard Bond

Paul Hamilton

Cartoons by Hamish MacDonald.

Printed in Toronto, Canada. The Strategic Coach Inc., 33 Fraser Avenue, Suite 201, Toronto, Ontario, M6K 3J9.

This publication is meant to strengthen your common sense, not to substitute for it. It is also not a substitute for the advice of your doctor, lawyer, accountant, or any of your advisors, personal or professional.

If you would like further information about the Strategic Coach® Program or other Strategic Coach® services and products, please telephone 416.531.7399 or 1.800.387.3206.

Library and Archives Canada Cataloguing in Publication

Sullivan, Dan, 1944-, author
Ambition scorecard / Dan Sullivan.

ISBN 978-1-897239-42-1 (paperback)

1. Entrepreneurship. 2. Ambition. I. Title.

HB615.S9435 2015 658.4'21 C2015-904943-1

Contents

Introduction

Surrounded By Ambition In 1966

When I was drafted into the U.S. Army in the 1960s, I spent most of my two years in South Korea. The South Korea of that time was a radically different country from the one we see today, which is a major economic power on the planet. Fifty years ago, it was a war-torn 18th-century country—poor, agriculturally-based, with little manufacturing.

I got to know quite a number of Koreans while I was there. Our base in Daegu was about 150 miles from the capital city of Seoul, and I remember that every time I rode the trains, the moment I sat down, there would be three or four Koreans who would immediately surround me.

They'd say, "Do you speak English? We've got three hours—can we speak English with you?"

I would ask the more advanced English speakers among them, "Why is this so important?" and they'd reply, "The whole world is going English, and our only ability to advance in our society is the speed with which we learn and master English."

Whether people like to admit it or not, English is the dominant language on the planet, and it takes a certain mindset to be motivated to master it. The South Koreans I met recognized that it was a capability that was absolutely crucial for their individual progress and development.

They had ambition, and they took every opportunity to give themselves an advantage. For me, they were a great example of individuals with their own *self-generated ambition.*

"WE NEED TO MASTER ENGLISH!"
AMBITION
PREDICTABLE
CONVENTIONAL
GOVERNMENT
EMPLOYERS
MEDIA
PEERS
TEACHERS
PARENTS
SELF-GENERATED

Conventional vs. self-generated ambition.

When I was in my teens in the 1950s, the word *ambition* had a very positive connotation. It was a desirable quality.

But today, the word *ambition* can cause negative reactions. Calling someone ambitious can carry with it suspicions about that person's values, and this often inspires resentment. For those whose value system is based on following a prescribed conventional path that was set out for them—by their parents, the education system, their peers, popular culture, the media, the job market, employers, corporate and government regulators, and so on—they don't want any outside competitors that might bypass everything they've worked for. They have good reason to feel this way.

There are growing examples over the last quarter-century of individuals with self-generated ambition who have bypassed the conventional career path and become billionaires—by being extraordinary 21st-century game changers.

And this has been viewed in a negative way by those whose sense of self and personal value have come entirely from their successes in following the path laid out for them by society. The successes of those who have made their way in the world outside of or despite these systems belie the claims about the importance of following the rules.

Individuals whose ambitions bypass the rules.

Self-generated ambition is not controllable from the outside. You can control people's conventional ambitions through grades, through social acceptance, and through decades of employment. But self-generated ambition, like my example of the Koreans on the train, cannot be controlled. These

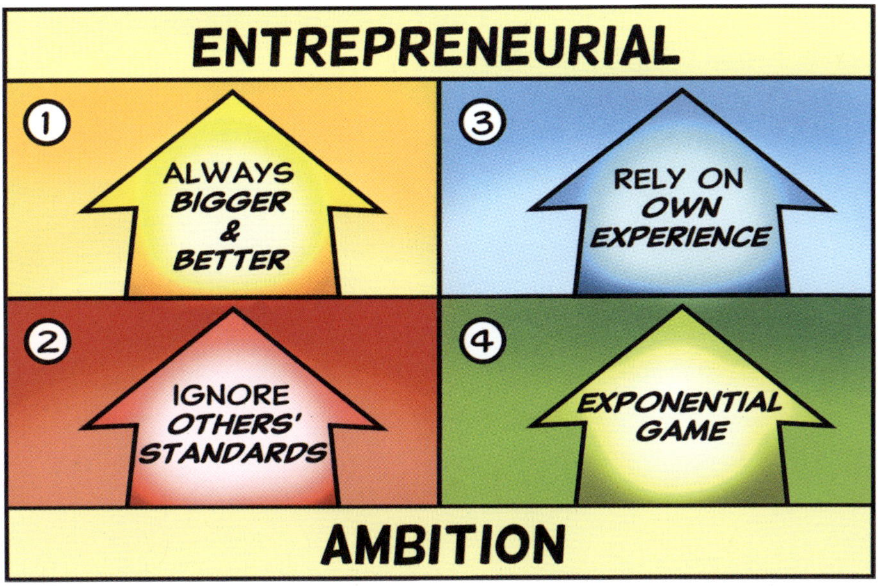

individuals create their own paths and follow their own rules.

This concept that anybody, regardless of their circumstances, can jump out of the conditions they are born in is very troublesome to people who have spent their entire lives playing by the rules. It's frustrating to them when somebody with a different kind of ambition either breaks the rules or ignores the rules and gets to the top anyway. And there's also another threat.

Five billion more competitors in just 70 years.

The global population was just slightly over two billion when I was born in 1944. Now, 70 years later, it's over seven billion. There is a sense of scarcity of opportunity on the part of the people who believe that their progress in life is going to be determined by going through a defined structure and playing by certain conventional rules. They're feeling a lot of pressure from their belief that there is not going to be enough opportunity to go around.

Someone who has their own self-generated ambitions, however, completely ignores all of that. They simply take advantage of their own sense of who they are and the unique opportunities they can create for themselves.

Identifying yourself as a multiplier entrepreneur.

Here I can substitute another term for taking a self-generated path and following self-generated rules in the 21st century:

Entrepreneurial ambition.

An entrepreneur is anyone who departs from the conventional formula, path, and rules for being successful. They are individuals who have the self-generated commitment, courage, capability, and confidence to make it on their own.

This book, however, is written specifically for those who are not only entrepreneurs, but who have already proven that they are talented and successful in creating their own futures according to their own uniquely self-generating ambition.

From my 40 years of coaching these entrepreneurial achievers, I have identified four crucial characteristics that set them apart. See if these are important to you:

1. They have always been self-motivated by a bigger and better future vision of themselves.

2. They increasingly ignore other people's standards and images of personal success.

3. Their own personal experience—including both wins and setbacks—has always been more useful and instructive to them than following other people's advice and examples.

4. They increasingly approach their entrepreneurial future as an exponential game that keeps jumping to higher levels of personal challenge, reward, and enjoyment.

Your Ambition Scorecard for making a 10x jump.

If these four characteristics describe you, you can take advantage of a shortcut we've created to speed up your next stage of entrepreneurial growth. It's called the Ambition Scorecard, and using it will multiply your self-generated ambition by 10x. The Scorecard takes everything that's made you a uniquely successful entrepreneur until now and uses it to accelerate growth in every area of your life.

Measurement

Telling The Truth To Multiply Your Progress

In World War II, there was a group of bright young men who controlled logistics for the U.S. Army Air Force. They developed innovative ways of getting armaments, fuel, and supplies to the air bases in Europe and the Pacific islands, ensuring that there were no delays in carrying out missions.

When the war ended, ten of these logistical experts had developed highly effective methods that could be applied to the civilian economy and, as a group, they hired themselves out to Ford Motor Company. The business press in America quickly called them the Whiz Kids.

Ford Motor's strange way of measuring.

Upon arriving at Ford, the Whiz Kids discovered that the company, which in 1945 was one of the most prominent corporations in the United States, determined their day-to-day bottom-line results in ways that would be considered very strange today.

The accountants and comptrollers at Ford Motor Company had figured out how to weigh receivables and payables by the pound—or, alternatively, how to measure them by the inch. They would determine whether the corporation was doing well by these crude measurements on a short-term basis during a business year, but it wasn't until six months after the end of the fiscal year that they got the actual data from their accounting firm.

That was considered normal procedure at Ford. Hardly anybody had up-to-date data because it was a big, widespread corporation that had a lot of reporting delays. Each department had their own receivables and payables. By the

STRANGE MEASURING
RECEIVED
PAID
GOOD YEAR
PAID
RECEIVED
BAD YEAR
6:00 7:00 8:00 9:00 10:00 11:00 12:00
RECEIVABLES
PAYABLES
REAL-TIME REPORTING
"THAT WHICH IS MEASURED *IMPROVES*."
"THAT WHICH IS MEASURED AND *REPORTED* IMPROVES *EXPONENTIALLY*."
- KARL PEARSON, MATHEMATICIAN & STATISTICIAN
PEARSON'S LAW

time all the information was collected for the corporation, it would take them a long time to see whether they had actually been profitable the previous year. By then, it was too late to make changes and improvements for that year.

What the Whiz Kids did was help the Ford Motor Company to create new, more sophisticated systems to manage the company and keep abreast of progress on a daily basis. Looking back, their solutions saved the company.

The "real time" reporting revolution.

Today, if you're the head of a large corporation and you don't know up to the minute what your balances are, you're running a really big risk. Companies operate in absolute real time now, and each year sees new measurement breakthroughs.

Between measuring results in pounds and inches in 1945 and operating in real time today, there have been millions and millions of improvements in measurement and scoring.

This has created a real time revolution in statistical measurement and reporting within business organizations throughout the global economy. In order to grow the capability and confidence of their companies, leaders have to tell the truth about their ongoing successes and failures. Otherwise, their employees, customers, and investors lose confidence and withdraw their engagement and support.

In the entire business universe, we're constantly striving for more and more accurate ways of measuring productivity and profitability. Our 21st-century world is one of measurement. And we have a man named Karl Pearson to thank for much of that progress.

Applying Pearson's Law to entrepreneurs.

Professor Pearson, an early 20th-century British mathematician who is considered the founder of the modern statistical methods that drive current business reporting, is credited with a powerfully simple "law": *"That which is measured improves. That which is measured and reported improves exponentially."*

Pearson's Law is now a universal operating principle for continually achieving any kind of progress on the planet for both organizations and individuals. Here's how I rephrase it so that it applies to everyone:

Those who measure their progress improve. Those who measure and report their progress improve exponentially.

Following this "law" is crucial for achieving increasingly greater personal and organizational success in the 21st-century entrepreneurial world.

Three kinds of entrepreneurs in the world.

Since I began coaching entrepreneurs in 1974, personally working with more than 6,000 individuals and their companies over the past four decades, I've identified three categories of entrepreneurs:

Survival Entrepreneurs: These individuals represent 90 percent of entrepreneurs and, essentially, they have simply created a job for themselves. They are self-employed. Their biggest motivation is to earn enough money to survive this year, and to have enough savings for retirement. These are generally their only goals and their only measurements of progress.

Lifestyle Entrepreneurs: Their entire motivation for being entrepreneurs is to create a personal lifestyle for themselves and their families that earns them respect, admiration, and greater security and comfort. They represent nine percent of entrepreneurs, and their most important measurements are in terms of achieving high social standing.

Ambition Entrepreneurs: This top one percent of entrepreneurs are continually motivated by their self-generated ambition over their entire lifetimes. Unlike those in the first two categories, ambition entrepreneurs never stop achieving. They are driven by a set of powerful mindsets that keep generating a greater ambition to develop and expand every area of their personal and professional achievement.

Focusing and growing your ambition mindsets.

In the next chapter, I introduce an entrepreneurial thinking tool called the Ambition Scorecard, which you'll find at the back of this book. (You can also download additional copies at strategiccoach.com/go/asc) The Scorecard represents an overall mindset measured by eight contributing mindsets. Within the one big concept of ambition, I've identified the eight most powerful mindsets that most contribute to having an ambition that constantly grows in a positive way for you and for everybody who's connected to you.

These mindsets don't define your ambition; rather, they're a lens through which you can continually measure and report on your entrepreneurial progress. *When you measure your ambition and report on it to other ambition entrepreneurs like you, it improves exponentially.*

Scorecard

All Ambition Starts With Mindset

Mindset determines everything. Having a particular mindset is choosing to look at the world in a particular way. You're betting on it: "If I look at the world this way, I'm going to get a huge payoff." The vast majority of people, however, don't choose their mindsets, and they don't know how their mindsets are restricting or preventing their ambition.

But this is not true for you—someone whose lifetime goal is the constant growth of personal ambition.

Since everything you do in the future as an ambition entrepreneur, and the way in which you look at your entrepreneurial past, is a function of your mindsets, let's clearly understand which mindsets are going to multiply your ambition.

Eight mindsets that multiply your ambition.

The Ambition Scorecard exercise is about choosing and strengthening the mindsets that have the biggest possible payoff for you in everything you're doing in life.

The eight mindsets I've identified, which make up the Scorecard, are the result of sorting through more than 100 different mindsets over the 40-year period that I've been coaching, listening to, interacting with, and responding to unusually ambitious entrepreneurs. They were developed in the 10x Ambition Program of Strategic Coach and are a way of thinking, communicating, and taking action you won't find anywhere outside of Strategic Coach.

I continually test these mindsets to determine whether each one really deserves to be one of the eight. Even with the eight we have, there may be another mindset that emerges that is

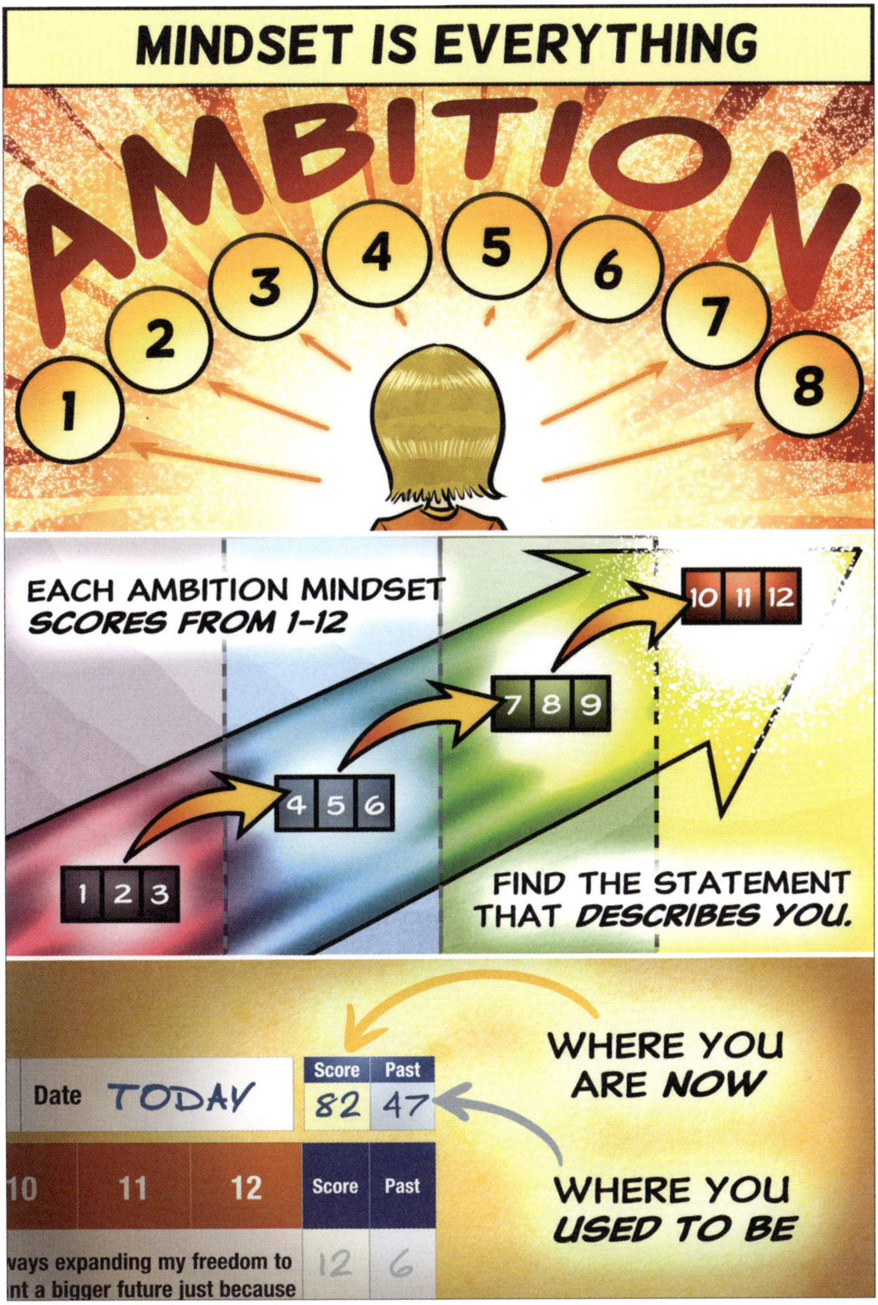
MINDSET IS EVERYTHING
AMBITION
1 2 3 4 5 6 7 8
EACH AMBITION MINDSET SCORES FROM 1–12
1 2 3
4 5 6
7 8 9
10 11 12
FIND THE STATEMENT THAT DESCRIBES YOU.
Date TODAY
Score Past
82 47
WHERE YOU ARE NOW
10 11 12 Score Past
vays expanding my freedom to
nt a bigger future just because
12 6
WHERE YOU USED TO BE

superior to one of them and will become a replacement for it. And keep in mind that the Scorecard is simply a way for you to look at your own ambition with these concepts in mind.

Here again, it's very useful to refer to the copy of the Scorecard exercise at the back of this book.

How to measure your ambition mindsets.

You'll notice that the Ambition Scorecard lists the eight mindsets down the left-hand side of the page. In the next columns are the criteria for each mindset with a series of four progressions—from not having these mindsets at all to being fully masterful of these mindsets. They're broken down into four quadrants and there is a scoring system across the top of the page.

1-12 Scoring: A score of one to three indicates that you don't have this mindset at all, and, as a matter of fact, might actually be opposed to this mindset. From four to six, you are a little bit in, but mostly out of the mindset. From seven to nine, you are mostly in the mindset, but not consistently. If you score in the fourth quadrant, 10 to 12, you are always in this mindset, and you keep developing and expanding it in every part of your life.

Choose the statement and score yourself.

For each of the mindsets, there are four statements. Choose the one that most relates to how you think, the one that operates most closely to how you generally communicate with other people and that generally describes how you act. Other people will more or less say this about you as well.

Your present score: Then choose one of the three numbers at

the top of the column that you feel best represents your score for that mindset. Write your score for each of the eight mindsets at the end of each row, and then write in your total score at the bottom of the Score column. This is your ambition mastery score. It represents your ambition levels right now.

Compare with a past score: The next step is to choose a point in your past—it could be 90 days ago, it could be three years ago, it could be when you first started as an entrepreneur—and in the second scoring column, score yourself on each mindset in the way you would have scored yourself back then.

What this does is give you a comparison that's meaningful to you—but meaningful only to you. This is a completely independent evaluation where only you can be the expert in this. The moment you have your score, it immediately becomes a starting line for improvement into the future.

Turning qualities into measurable quantities.

The power of the Scorecard is that it starts off totally qualitative and subjective. In other words, I don't know what's going on in another person's mind when they're reading the Scorecard. I don't know what experiences they're relating to. I do know that the words mean a great deal to them. I also know that the words relate to very powerful experiences they've had. I know that if I give them the choice of this number or that number, they can immediately choose the number that most relates to them.

The Scorecard takes your powerful qualitative experience of entrepreneurial ambition and enables you to measure it as a highly motivating number.

The difference between this scoring system and a more metric-based one is that this one is about mindset, which is much different than your income statement or your bank balance. This is how you're thinking, how you're feeling, how you're responding to your world and your own definition of how you measure ambition.

Improving to achieve a "12" in every mindset.

As you make continual progress with your Ambition Scorecard—I recommend using it every 90 days—you'll discover three things:

- **You'll always want to go higher:** The human brain is hardwired to love and respond to scoring. The moment you have a number, you'll want it to go up.

• **Let yourself achieve a "12":** The Ambition Scorecard is totally geared to your 90-day improvements, and if you have a huge improvement in a mindset area that deserves a 12, let yourself have it. As soon as you get your first 12 in one mindset, you'll be totally motivated to get 12s in the other seven ambition mindsets as well.

• **Your standards keep going up:** As soon as you achieve your first 12 in a particular mindset, you will immediately raise your standards for achieving a score of 12 during the next 90 days.

Now that you have a handle on how the Scorecard works, let's explore the powerful impact of each of the eight mind-sets that can continually multiply your overall ambition for the rest of your life.

Mindset 1:
Wanting What You Want

The mindset of Wanting What You Want came to me in 1978 when I was both divorced and bankrupt on the same day. One of the decisions I made that day was that, from then on, for the next 25 years, I would be sure to tell myself every day what I really wanted in order to avoid being in that kind of situation again.

The key aspect of wanting—versus needing—is that with wanting, you don't have to justify what you want. There is no need for the word "because." This liberating skill of wanting frees you from having to justify your ambitions.

There are four key distinctions between wanting and needing. First, needing has external sources, whereas wanting, like ambition, is internal. For wanters, their goals come from the inside. The second distinction is that needs relate to a sense of security, while wants are motivated by freedom. Third, needers are operating from a mindset of scarcity. Wanters, on the other hand, see the world as a place of abundance and recognize all the opportunities to create what they want. The fourth distinction is that the needing world is always reacting to constantly changing situations, but the wanting world is creative and full of innovators.

Big "wanting" grows big ambition.

Each of these "wanting" distinctions supports your self-generated ambition. Having an ambition mindset means that you are free to want a bigger future without having to justify wanting it to anyone else.

When it comes to ambition, it's necessary to give up the thought that you need to get permission to do what you want

AMBITION ENTREPRENEURS...
EXTERNAL
SECURITY
SCARCITY
REACTIVE
NEEDING
WANTING
INTERNAL
FREEDOM
ABUNDANCE
CREATIVE
...ARE WANTERS
NEEDING
WANTING
JUSTIFICATION
NO JUSTIFICATION
WELL, SEE, I NEED THIS BECAUSE...
AND I FEEL BAD THAT...
I COME FROM...
I ONLY ASK SINCE...
I'M NOT VERY...
SORRY!
SORRY!
AMBITION MINDSET:
THE REASON WHY YOU WANT IT IS
BECAUSE YOU WANT IT!

to do. The moment you get the notion that any move forward on your part requires someone else's permission, approval, or even support, you have to then spend an enormous amount of energy to get their approval and to justify why you want it. The truth of the matter is that there is only one explanation for why you want something: You want it because you want it. Wanting is its own self-propelling activity.

A lot of people who grow up in a world where their progress has always been dependent upon someone else's permission or approval never develop this "wanting" part of their brains. They really don't have the mindset that they can base their entire life on higher and higher levels of wanting. But this kind of ambition doesn't require anyone else's approval.

It does, however, require other people's teamwork. And with the Wanting What You Want mindset, you become highly selective of who gets to be on your team.

Needing others' approval is a scarcity trap.

The opposite of the world of wanting is one where everything is based on needs, where other people are in control of all the factors that are going to allow you to satisfy your needs. In the needing realm, your whole life is geared toward being popular or being compliant and obedient—you are constantly in the mode of being worried about other people's opinions of you, other people's judgments about you. So all of your thinking, which could be devoted to creativity, is used up in interpersonal politics.

Entrepreneurs who come from a place of need are trapped in a scarcity mindset where they can feel resentful and intimidated by the success and advantages of others. Or

they may feel guilty about their own success when other people in their life aren't as successful.

Ambition and success need no justification.

A lot of entrepreneurs also feel that the only way to justify their success is to "give back" in the form of charity or by helping their community. Philanthropic endeavors are noble gestures that should always be lauded, but the idea that being successful requires you to "give back" implies that there is something you have taken. Rather than aiming to "give back" so you can justify your success, recognize that your success requires no justification and, instead, give for giving's sake.

Exponential entrepreneurs want a bigger and better future

just because they want it, with no need whatsoever to justify their continual progress and success. Being able to give generously to others is one of the great rewards of success, not an obligation.

Wanting is the starting point for ambition.

Ambitious people tend to hang out with ambitious people, and they tend to attract to their teams people who are also ambitious for their own reasons. They like the idea of being in a community of ambitious people.

What's notable about ambition entrepreneurs in any area of activity is the absence of any notion on their part that they need anyone else's permission to move forward on their vision of personal progress.

The Wanting What You Want mindset is the center of ambition. It's the decision that, throughout your life, you're going to move forward toward what you want. Whether other people support this or approve of it is something you may have to deal with as a strategy or a bypass, but it has nothing to do with whether you're going to do it.

Ambition entrepreneurs never think in terms of scarcity because their experience in life is that anything they wanted, they triggered with their own intelligence and in teamwork with other ambitious, creative people.

Self-generating comes from self-scoring.

The statement that gets you the highest score on the Ambition Scorecard is wanting a bigger future without a need to justify why you want it. When you're scoring yourself on this first ambition mindset, ask yourself whether

you're only as successful as you *need* to be or whether you're as success as you *want* to be.

Best possible mindset: Ambition entrepreneurs didn't get to where they are just so they could compare themselves to others. The people who do this are lifestyle entrepreneurs. But if you are someone who self-generates your ambition by Wanting What You Want, then you only compare yourself to how you were previously. You are self-scoring. The vast majority of human beings take their scoring from other people's opinions, but ambition entrepreneurs like you take their scoring from the inside. You have your own internal checklist of whether you are moving forward or not moving forward. That's why wanting is so powerful—it gets you started with the best possible ambition mindset right from the beginning.

Mindset 2:
The 25-Year Framework

Back in 1978, when I went through my divorce and bankruptcy, I felt very strongly that one of the biggest reasons for the two failures was that I had incorrect mindsets—namely, that I was thinking only about the next day or the next week.

So here is how I resolved to correct that: I would focus on the one ability of Wanting What I Want and writing this down in a journal every day for 25 years. I could write whole pages or paragraphs, but at least a single sentence. I felt that if I simply went through this daily activity for 25 years, which is 100 quarters, every mindset that led to the divorce and bankruptcy would be transformed, and I would have a completely different mindset. As it turns out, that was true.

Not only did I achieve my goal, I achieved something even more powerful and lasting:

I developed the capability to see "sticking with something for 25 years" as the best way of looking at my time ahead.

This has been an amazing mindset for me, and it is the second component of the Ambition Scorecard.

Investing now in 25-year multiplier capabilities.

Many entrepreneurs in today's marketplace are looking only at short-term goals. They're thinking short-range because they're worried about decreasing cash flow and profits. They continually cut back on expenses in order to keep their businesses going, then to save for their retirement. Again, these are the survival and lifestyle entrepreneurs I described earlier.

STICKING WITH SOMETHING
FAILURE 1
FAILURE 2
1978
25 YEARS
100 QUARTERS
2003
TOTALLY DIFFERENT MINDSET
ANXIETY
PRESSURE
STRESS
MULTIPLIERS
SHORT-TERM
25 YEARS
ALL THE TIME IN THE WORLD!
WINNING
LEARNING

Even ambition entrepreneurs who are operating without an Ambition Scorecard can get caught up in this short-range mentality, concerned with maximizing their revenues because they're not certain about where their ambition will take them next. This is understandable and prudent, but The 25-Year Framework is a much more powerful mindset. Indeed, the longer the time period you can plan ahead, the more you can make continual progress that multiplies itself.

If you operate from an ambition mindset that each 90 days represents just one percent of 25 years, you will increasingly invest in opportunities that multiply your capability exponentially.

Relaxing because you have lots of time.

I've found when working with entrepreneurs in The 10x Program, they start getting frustrated by their lack of short-term progress. When I tell them that the overall goal and strategy is for 25 years and that this is just one week out of one quarter—and the quarter is only one percent of 25 years—suddenly, their anxiety is gone.

Transforms perspective: The 25-Year Framework induces profound and immediate relaxation in entrepreneurs who have never been relaxed about time in their lives. It changes their perspective, and they see that they can do a lot more in their future than they thought was possible. Before, they didn't think they had enough time for their biggest goals, and now they see that they have more than enough time.

Only winning and learning: Within a 25-year framework, there is no room for frustration and failure. There are only two possibilities for experience in this 25-year period:

You're either winning or you're learning. Having a 25-year mindset gives you a different perspective on the future and what you're capable of achieving in that future.

Eliminates anxiety: The framework takes away the anxiety that comes from feeling that you have to get everything done in the short-term. If you think of your ambition only in regard to the short-term, then there are 100 things you have to get done in the next quarter.

Your future expands: If, on the other hand, you have a sense that the 90 days ahead constitute just one percent of a bigger 25-year framework, there are just a few things you have to get done in the next quarter. Suddenly, your time and your future expand. You realize that you are not dealing with an external "time reality" that limits you. You are dealing only with an internal reality that's strictly based on how you look ahead.

A mindset that's the opposite of retirement.

Another limiting mindset that undermines ambition is the concept of retirement—and it's a particularly self-defeating viewpoint for entrepreneurs. It's important to understand that retirement age in any society is actually for people who work for somebody else. It does not apply to those who create their own organizations.

Retirement is a strictly bureaucratic concept. It has nothing to do with entrepreneurial life. Implicit in the mindset of retirement is that your work life is not really the life you'd like to be leading, that your ideal life doesn't involve anything to do with your work. For entrepreneurs, however, it's being discovered that their work is more stimulating and more motivating to them than any other activity they do in their lives.

Very few entrepreneurs feel that when they stop working, their life afterward can compare in any way to the enjoyment and the sense of personal value and significance they felt while they were working. This is because, to the world at large, they don't count anymore. To retire means to be taken out of use, and retirement puts you in a position where you no longer matter.

Totally motivated: The 25-Year Framework is just the opposite of retirement. When people retire, they stop measuring, and they stop scoring. And this means they stop improving. When you're planning and growing with 25 years in mind, you increasingly improve all along the way, and you're totally motivated to measure and score your perfor-

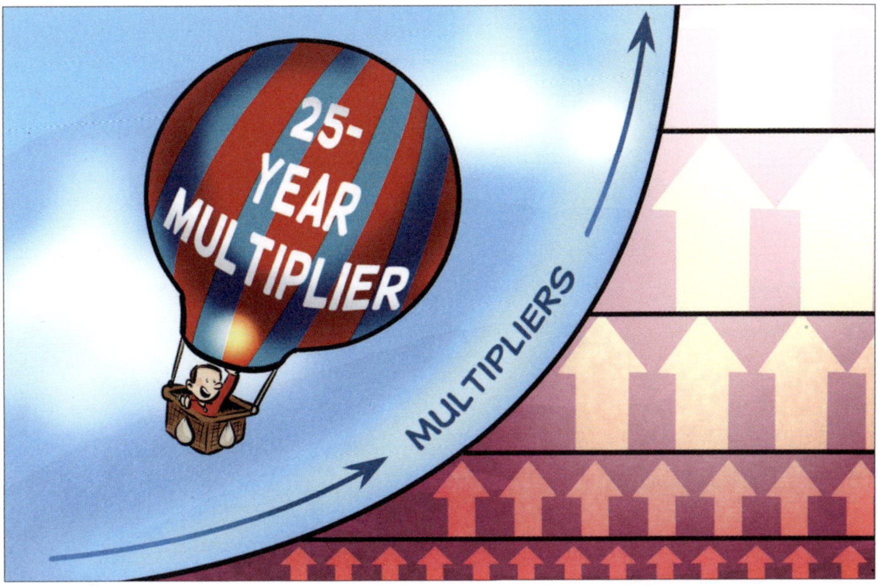

mance at the end of each of the 100 quarters.

The friendliest time multiplier in the world.
The longer your time frame, the more willing you'll be to invest in something that will pay off months and years down the road. When you continually expand The 25-Year Framework as a crucial component of your ambition mindset, you'll find that you look at every achievement as an investment, and every investment as an achievement.

The friendliest mindset in the world is one where you feel that everything you're doing today will increasingly have a greater multiplier impact in the future—that everything you do today will continually multiply over the next 25 years.

Mindset 3:
The 10x Mindset

The world in which we're living is increasingly based on microchip-empowered technology, and we're seeing more and more examples of exponential progress. Companies are going from zero to a billion dollars in radically short periods of time.

For most people, the notion of how quickly you can grow as an individual as well as how quickly an organization can expand is still seen in terms of a historic model where things could only be done incrementally. Now, we're getting a lot of proof—and it's very disruptive proof—that things can change very quickly. Growth can happen very quickly.

With the right ambition mindset, you can multiply your entrepreneurial progress 10x. 10x can mean many different things. It can be in terms of income or profits or how well you're known. It could be in terms of your network of connections or your capabilities.

In Strategic Coach, we measure 10x in terms of your entrepreneurial freedom, specifically in terms of Time, Money, Relationship, and Purpose.

Time: Getting things done faster
It's now possible to get an incredible number of things done in very short periods of time because technology speeds up processes and also gives you access to other people's capabilities. This allows you to build a team around you at a remarkably low cost, freeing up even more time. People are now realizing they can accomplish the same amount of work in less time, with time left over to do whatever they want. That's an enormous growth of freedom.

EVERYTHING'S MULTIPLYING
10X
10X
10X
10X
10X
10X
10X
10X
10X
10X
10X
TIME
MONEY
RELATIONSHIP
PURPOSE
ENTREPRENEURIAL FREEDOM
10X FASTER
10X CHEAPER
10X EASIER
10X BIGGER

Money: Bigger results with less effort

If you're creating something that's of value to a great number of people and using technology as the means for delivering it, you can make a lot of money with far less effort than what's been true historically. We're getting a proliferation of examples of people with very powerful mindsets about how this new world works who are training themselves to have the skills and the knowledge necessary to take advantage of exponential growth, giving them no limit to how much money they can make.

Relationship: Bigger like-minded networks

You can now have relationships everywhere on the planet. They can cross borders. They can cross cultures. More and more, I see these relationships being based on like-mindedness and complementary skills. You're no longer confined to where you were born or the economic circumstances you were born into. People have a freedom now to create networks of relationships that don't have much to do with where they came from, but have more to do with where they're going.

Purpose: Thinking global, reaching billions

I have an immediate goal of getting my previous book, *The 4 C's Formula*, into the hands of a billion people, which, today, can be done electronically. What that gives me is a 10x purpose. Never in my life before this have I thought about impacting a billion people and have actually had a very practical focus to achieve that. Because I have a 10x Mindset, I see that it's possible.

Growing 10x is easier than trying for 2x.

What we see in the world is a division of mindsets between

people who can think 10x and people who think in terms of incremental progress. With an incremental mindset, progress is very modest, very slow, and very hard. But those with a 10x Mindset see that things could happen very fast, could be really easy, could be a lot cheaper, and could bring a much bigger result.

When you think in terms of 10x, it forces you to decide what you're really good at and focus only on those things. You immediately take a look at your past and make a very clear judgment about how much of it is supportive of a 10x goal, and what is best left behind.

If, on the other hand, your goal is only to make a 50 percent improvement, you might try to do it the same way you've done it before. Even the person aiming for 2x is wondering how little change they can get away with and still double their growth. There's a temptation with a goal less than 10x to pull it off without any real personal or organizational change.

The spectrum from reactive to exponential.

Those at the incremental end of the spectrum—the opposite of 10x—are not looking at the future at all; they're looking at the past. They're regretting mistakes, bad decisions, and lost opportunities. They're obsessed with what's already happened, and they're backing into the future.

Just holding on: A little further to the right on the Scorecard is where someone is just trying to take the best of what they've done in the past and see if they can maintain it going into the future. A lot of people are playing a defensive game in life. They've secured some success and now, for the rest of their lives, they're just going to try to protect what they've secured. This requires an enormous amount of non-productive energy.

Maintaining is not natural for entrepreneurs. Striving and growing is natural. That's where the most positive energy, excitement, and meaning come from.

Trapped by average success: The next step up the Scorecard is aiming to grow by 10 percent per year, doubling every ten years. There is nothing wrong with that, but it's not exciting in the 21st century. Indeed, extreme setbacks are often better than satisfaction with mediocrity. It's the traps of success that are much harder to get out of than the traps of failure. This is because built into failure is a motivation to transform yourself, but built into success is a motivation to just keep doing what you're doing.

Exchanging a heavier past for a lighter future.

Growing 10x means that you examine everything you're doing from top to bottom and determine that you have to get very lightweight in your thinking and performance, which means leaving a lot of your past behind. Survival entrepreneurs never think this way, and lifestyle entrepreneurs have no reason to. But as an ambition entrepreneur, your mind is always looking toward a bigger and better future for yourself and your organization.

The moment you start thinking 10x, you start noticing every opportunity that offers 10x, every capability that offers 10x, every resource that offers 10x, and every relationship that offers 10x. As this mindset becomes more powerful, you take greater advantage of the very best possibilities for expanding your overall ambition.

Mindset 4:

The Moving Future Mastery

A very successful entrepreneur in the 10x Ambition Program was having a hard time achieving a breakthrough. He was using an old way of thinking about time and progress, and saying he needed a five-year plan for where he was going to take his business.

I said to him, "Tell me how much you've accomplished in the last year that you could have predicted a year ago."

He replied, "Well, I couldn't have predicted 80 percent of what's happened."

I said, "Then what's a five-year plan going to do for you? Since you couldn't predict what was going to happen 12 months ahead, how much added value will come from five years?"

I added, "What you need is a 'moving future,' not a fixed future."

90-day clarity with one mindset tool.

From this one conversation, I created a new thinking exercise in Strategic Coach called The Moving Future. With this mindset tool, you look at four things: your winning achievements over the previous 90 days, what's making you confident right now, what's giving you the greatest sense of excitement over the next 90 days, and the next five big achievements to focus on. Here is a breakdown of these four components:

Morale: What you're proud of

As soon as you start using The Moving Future, you'll have an increased sense of morale for your upcoming 90 days

THE MOVING FUTURE
90 DAYS
5 YEARS
AMBITION CLARITY IN 12 MINUTES
MORALE
MOMENTUM
MOTIVATION
MULTIPLIERS
PRIDE
CONFIDENCE
EXCITEMENT
BREAKTHROUGHS

based on your winning achievements from your previous 90 days. After two minutes of thinking about the business and personal progress you've achieved, and writing this down, you get a sudden burst of pride. Immediately, your mind jumps into the present, and you get excited about the future because you now know there is nothing else in your recent past you need to spend time thinking about.

Momentum: What you're confident about
Now, with your mind freed up from the the past, you can focus your attention for the next two minutes on the current areas of activity where you and your company are experiencing the greatest progress—in other words, everything you're most energized by and where your greatest achievements can happen most quickly. As soon as you write down five or six items, your confidence takes a jump, and when this happens, you are now ready to focus entirely on the future. At this point, you've spent a total of four minutes on your Moving Future.

Motivation: What you're excited about
You've now transformed your past into high morale, and your present into a powerful sense of momentum. It's time to multiply your sense of excitement about the future. Because of your greater sense of pride and confidence that has been created so far, new things suddenly appear on the horizon as possibilities for even greater progress and achievement over the next 90 days. The emotion here is a powerful excitement that will come from five or six new initiatives you'll get started on over the next quarter. Once you've spent two minutes writing these down, sit back and look at the extraordinary and empowering information you've gathered in only six minutes.

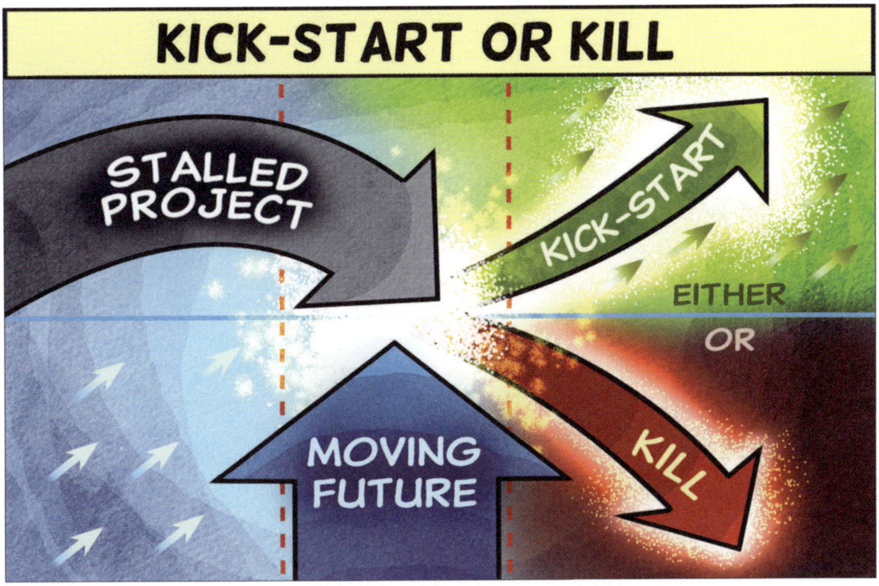

Multipliers: Five 25-year breakthrough projects
Something remarkable happens at this point in The Moving Future exercise. From all that you've written, your mind can now distill everything down to just five "breakthrough projects" you can complete by the end of the next quarter, and each one of these projects will continually grow for the next 25 years. Think about this whole exercise in terms of compound interest: You plant new capabilities in the near future that will continually multiply themselves for the rest of your entrepreneurial career.

Jump-starting stalled projects—or not.

The Moving Future exercise is a very fast thinking process. In about 12 minutes, you can sum up your last 90 days, where you are now, what's coming in the next 90 days, as well as the five things to focus the majority of your investible energy and skill on over the next 90 days. You can train yourself on a daily basis to be looking only for those things that have the highest possibility of morale, momentum, motivation, and multipliers.

When I'm working on a project and I find that it's losing energy, I'll stop and say, "Over the next 12 minutes, I'm going to do one of two things: I'm either going to restore maximum energy to this project or, if it looks like it's not worth it, I'm going to cut the project off." It's a 100 percent yes or 100 percent no. There's nothing more energy-draining than to be in the situation of "maybe."

With The Moving Future, you make clear-cut decisions, focus yourself clearly, and throw yourself into things completely. Because of the short, 90-day time frames, you're able to constantly adjust to changing circumstances. It's the perfect planning tool for ambition entrepreneurs and their teams in a 21st-century world that's based on the unpredictable change being caused by technology.

Adjusting each 90 days to the next 25 years.

We no longer have fixed futures. The continual, fluid change we're living in requires a totally different way of structuring time in our minds. On the one hand, we need a clear focus toward which we can throw all our energy for a given time, but at the same time, we need enough flexibility that if the world changes, we can change the game plan.

With my 25-Year Framework, I have a set plan for how I'm going to be when I'm in my nineties. This plan hasn't changed much at all since I first decided on it three years ago. But I reword the specific plans on a continual basis.

When I get to the end of 25 years, you'll be able to track my accomplishments to something I said 25 years previously. But having established a 25-year certainty and predictability for myself, I can then be totally flexible *within* the 25 years.

The 90-day time frames of The Moving Future allow you to course-correct along the way to your 25-year goals.

You can confidently focus on the next 90 days, and you can be totally committed to your next 25 years. But it isn't worth trying to predict anything in between. The 90 days is for continual flexibility, and the 25 years is for reinforcement.

With The Moving Future, you skillfully and continually recalibrate your focus every 90 days on the basis of always increasing morale, momentum, motivation, and multipliers.

Mindset 5:
The 4 C's Formula

There are eight mindsets discussed in this book that make up the larger ambition mindset. But if you could focus on only one of them to create a bigger and better entrepreneurial future, it would be this fifth one, The 4 C's Formula.

The 4 C's stands for an integrated growth process of Commitment, Courage, Capability, and Confidence.

If you look at each one of the significant breakthroughs that brought you to your present level of success, you'll notice that each of these achievements can be reconstructed in terms of the 4 C's.

Whether you know it or not, every time you put these four activator skills together, you were successful.

And by the same token, all of your entrepreneurial failures and frustrations occurred when you were lacking one or more of the components of this formula. Put simply, everything that's worth remembering about your entrepreneurial career to this point can be explained by the 4 C's, and every greater ambition that you have for the future can be constructed on the basis of the 4 C's.

The simple formula that always grows ambition.

Let's go through the four stages of how your ambition grows to see why each one is so necessary.

1. Commitment: Commitment means completely buying into a vision of a bigger and better future for yourself and being willing to start taking action toward achieving that vision—*before you have the capability and confidence that*

BUILDING BLOCKS OF AMBITION
4 CONFIDENCE
1 COMMITMENT
2 COURAGE
3 CAPABILITY
AMBITION OR FRUSTRATION
COMMITMENT COMM
COURAGE COUR
COMMITMENT
COURAGE
COMM
AVOIDANCE
PROCRASTINATION
BAD HABITS
ADDICTION
AMBITION
COURAGE CREATES CAPABILITY

will come from the achievement.

2. Courage: The courage stage is where your unfitness and unpreparedness for that future breakthrough impact on you psychologically and emotionally. *And you move forward anyway.* You're committed, but at the same time, you have an awareness of how much you're lacking and how much you're deficient in actually being able to pull off the goal you've committed to, which generates fear.

But the fact that you feel scared doesn't mean you haven't made a great or worthwhile commitment. It simply means that in order to pull off what you've committed to doing, you have to persevere and go through a period of courage.

The more you can treat feeling uncertain, uncomfortable, and fearful in relationship to a big commitment as normal, the greater your ongoing creation of new capabilities and the higher your levels of confidence will be.

3. Capability: The first two C's create the focus, energy, and sense of urgency necessary for the third C to emerge. Simply put: Commitment x Courage = Capability. All innovation on the planet, in every field of activity, comes from individuals who are willing to operate in the scary and exciting space between Courage and Capability—both of which have been set up by big Commitments.

4. Confidence: You've made the Commitment, you've gone through the period of Courage, and in doing this, you've created an entirely new Capability. Now comes your payoff for being more committed, courageous, and capable: Confidence. Every time you create a new capability in any

area of your life, you immediately experience a jump in your personal confidence.

Everybody can learn this process in ten minutes.

The 4 C's process is deceptively simple but amazingly powerful, and there are very few individuals who cannot understand and learn how to use it successfully in a matter of minutes. That's why this one ambition mindset is so important to the other seven that make up the Ambition Scorecard.

For example, let's apply the 4 C's to the first mindset, Wanting What You Want. On a sheet of paper, draw the 4 C's boxes as illustrated at the beginning of this chapter, leaving space for your notes in each box. Then write down what you want in the form of a commitment in box number one. As soon as you do this, you'll become aware of the fears and uncertainties you associate with this commitment. Write two or three of these fears in the second box, "Courage." Then in box three, visualize and write down the new capability you're going to create by being courageous while following through on your commitment. Finally, to complete the formula, describe the reason you will have higher confidence as result of creating this new capability.

At most, this will take you ten minutes to finish. You'll immediately go into action and surprise yourself by how quickly you can achieve your desired result. Every time you use The 4 C's Formula to achieve what you want in any area of your life, your entrepreneurial ambition will get bigger and better.

Use the 4 C's to raise *all* your ambition scores. Looking back at Mindset 1, you can see that the path to achieving what you want is simpler and easier when you make the commitment and go through the courage phase. Continually going through The 4 C's Formula is also the ideal way to build your bigger and better progress over the next 100 quarters, or 25 years.

And since you're going to be making this bigger and better progress, why not use a 10x Mindset to commit to making each of your new achievements 10x bigger and better? You can do this by setting up everything in the form of the four stages of commitment, courage, capability, and confidence.

Within each of those 100 quarters, you can use the Moving Future planning structure to identify your five biggest multiplier projects and breakthroughs. Each of these quarterly breakthroughs is the perfect focus for using your 4 C's Formula.

Transforming fear into positive raw material.

Ambition entrepreneurs are different from other individuals in many ways, but the biggest difference lies in how they courageously think about and respond to the fears that are automatically triggered by their increasing ambitions. Most people think that fear means that something is wrong with them, that something is wrong with their ambitions, and so they don't move forward to try to achieve them.

But successful people see fears and obstacles as a beginning, not an end. Ambition entrepreneurs look at fear as the crucial raw material that provides them with the transformative energy and urgency to enable them to break through to powerful new capabilities that trigger higher levels of personal confidence. Using The 4 C's Formula is the way to make these breakthroughs increasingly possible.

Mindset 6:
The Self-Multiplying Company

In my 10x workshops at Strategic Coach, I'll write the words "Self-Multiplying Company" on the white board, and then ask the question:

"Even if you don't know exactly what I mean by this, how many of you want one of these?"

All of the ambition entrepreneurs in the room instantly and enthusiastically raise their hands. The discussion that follows this question proves over and over again that one of the most powerful entrepreneurial daydreams is having a company that grows itself.

Everything starts by expanding four freedoms.

At the center of a Self-Multiplying Company is an individual who is a consciously self-multiplying person, and this multiplication comes through the expansion of the Four Freedoms of Time, Money, Relationship, and Purpose. An entrepreneur continually multiplies the power and impact of their life by this constant expansion of personal freedom.

Unique Ability: Key to The Self-Multiplying Company is Unique Ability. Unique Ability is a combination of your passion and unique talents—what you love to do and do best. It's a set of activities, usually no more than three, that provide a lifetime of fascination and motivation for you. There are three characteristics of a Unique Ability activity:

- **Passion:** You are always fascinated and motivated by doing this, you always have been, and 25 years from now, this will be even truer.

WHAT EVERYONE WANTS
WHO WANTS A
SELF-MULTIPLYING COMPANY
WHERE SELF-MULTIPLYING STARTS
UNIQUE ABILITY
PASSION
HERO
MULTIPLIERS
CREATIVITY
CAPABILITY
CREDIBILITY
PURPOSE
RELATIONSHIP
MONEY
TIME
UNIQUE ABILITY
TIME
MONEY
RELATIONSHIP
PURPOSE
SELF-MULTIPLYING COMPANY
SELF-MULTIPLYING COMPANY
CONNECTIONS
CONFIDENCE
CASH
OUTWARD EXPANSION

• **Hero:** You are totally motivated to do this activity in order to help a particular kind of person in the world transform their particular situation in uniquely creative ways.

• **Multipliers:** As an ambition entrepreneur, you are increasingly rewarded for your passion and for being a hero in six ways that keep becoming more powerful: greater capabilities, creativity, credibility, connections, confidence, and cash (revenues and profits).

Self-Multiplying Company develops & expands.

When you're focused on your Unique Ability activities and on expanding your freedoms of Time, Money, Relationship, and Purpose, you also organize your teamwork, both within your company and with the outside world, in such a way that every improvement in the organization expands your personal freedom, and every expansion of your personal freedom expands your organization.

It's a never-ending reciprocal process that enables everyone else in your process to develop and expand their Unique Ability and teamwork.

"Batteries included": When each person in your organization is operating within their area of Unique Ability, you're freed up to focus on innovation and creating the vision for your company. Not only that, but when everyone is working in their area of passion and energy, there is little need for supervision or micromanagement—everyone has "batteries included." This means that they are self-motivated, self-managing, and self-monitoring, which produces an organization that is continually self-multiplying.

Employees rewarded for being self-multiplying. Three or four generations ago, in the world of industrial bureaucracies, companies would operate with distinct levels of supervision and management, and the most successful employees were those who could be the most machine-like, particularly in factory or office settings.

But what people are being asked to do now is to be fully human. This means being creative and providing unique value based on their individual talents and skills. They're being asked to take what they have and multiply it.

Everyone in your company has the opportunity to be an entrepreneur in relationship to their daily situation. It's no longer good enough in the marketplace to just produce a predictable result. Now, people are being asked to produce an unpredictable result that's better than what existed before. The more this happens inside of your organization, the more your company is self-multiplying.

In your Self-Multiplying Company, your team sees that they're going to be rewarded not only for being alert, curious, responsive, and resourceful, but for taking processes in the company and making them faster, easier, and cheaper and for getting bigger results.

Your company self-generates new capabilities.

When your company no longer has just one creative person, but several, the responsibility for creativity and growth starts to multiply outward. With more and more team members in a creative role in the company, you cross the threshold into an expanding Unique Ability network that continually generates new capabilities, resources, and opportunities.

The big breakthrough here is that this expansion and growth increasingly happen without your needing to be personally involved. This is one of the greatest goals of ambition entrepreneurs: to have your own Self-Multiplying Company.

You're in charge. Everyone else is in control.

Going back to the three categories of entrepreneurs—survival, lifestyle, and ambition—the first two have a permanent goal of being in control of everything in their organization. This means that nothing can develop or expand without their direct involvement, and that most of their time and energy is increasingly taken up with existing activities.

This is not the case for ambition entrepreneurs. As you continually establish, strengthen, and combine your ambi-

tion multipliers, you automatically create a Self-Multiplying Company in which you are increasingly able to be in charge of future growth because everyone else is increasingly in control of maximizing your current capabilities and opportunities.

Being in charge means introducing maximum energy and electricity into the situation. It means that you're in charge of innovating new ideas and solutions, and of setting the context for the future growth of the organization.

Your Self-Multiplying Company, as you continually expand it, makes it possible for you personally to jump to higher levels of personal achievement and confidence. And every time you do this, you'll discover entirely new ways to increase your measurements on your Ambition Scorecard.

Mindset 7:

The Game Changer

Imagine right now that you have mastered the first six ambition mindsets in this book. You operate every day on the basis of (1) "wanting what you want" and do this within (2) a 25-year framework where all your progress is aimed at (3) 10x breakthroughs that are so energizing that your quarters, even though they are just one percent of 25 years, are increasingly measured in terms of (4) increasing morale, momentum, motivation, and multiplier achievements.

And all of this movement forward is extraordinarily clear and simple for you and the team around you because all new initiatives are taking place (5) within a continually strengthening formula of greater commitment, courage, capability, and confidence (6) and within an organization that is constantly expanding and self-multiplying.

All of this says that you have become a Game Changer.

How does this affect your competitors?

As you and your company develop and expand in the six extraordinary ways described above, here is how it will affect your biggest competitors regardless of the industry or marketplace in which you're operating:

Increasingly confused: Because they can't see your mindsets, they don't understand how you are improving.

Disturbed by change: Somebody has changed the game, but they don't know what the new rules are.

Feeling bypassed: There's a new message and method in the marketplace, and they don't know what to say or do.

YOU TAKE A SUDDEN JUMP
WANTING WHAT YOU WANT
THE 25-YEAR FRAMEWORK
10X MINDSET
SELF-MULTIPLYING COMPANY
THE 4 C'S FORMULA
MOVING FUTURE MASTERY
YOUR COMPETITORS GET DISRUPTED
INCREASINGLY CONFUSED
SUDDENLY ALERT
ANXIOUS TO LEARN
DISTURBED BY CHANGE
MOTIVATED TO TRANSFORM
FEELING BYPASSED
INNOVATIVE TEAMWORK
NEW GAMES START WITH NEW MINDSETS
NEW MINDSETS
NEW TECHNOLOGY
NEW TEAMWORK
NEW MARKETS

Suddenly alert: They wake up to the fact that if they don't change their thinking, they're going to be left behind.

Anxious to learn: They come to you as potential students because you are clearly doing something bigger and better.

Motivated to transform: They become your best customers and promoters because they see that you're creating a new, bigger game for everyone.

Innovative teamwork: Your change of game inspires them to change their own game, and their transformation, in turn, inspires you to make your ambition even bigger.

Uber's game is changing everyone's game.

For an example of a present day Game Changer, consider the remarkable success of Uber and how they've revolutionized the transportation industry by developing an app that connects drivers with customers. Because the Uber innovation starts with a completely different series of mindsets about transportation, it has created an extraordinarily bigger and better value proposition around the world.

But the biggest significance of Uber isn't actually Uber itself—it's that going forward, there will be millions of Uber-like Game Changers in every industry and marketplace in our 21st-century world.

All of these Game Changers represent ambition entrepreneurs who want to expand their personal freedoms. All of them create uniquely different kinds of mindsets that bypass their competition, and they operate with new kinds of advanced technology to create higher levels of marketplace teamwork.

These entrepreneurs have jumped to another level in terms of how they create value. They rewrite the rules on how to succeed in a particular industry and, in doing so, create entirely new marketplaces.

Moreover, by changing the rules, they greatly increase the amount of teamwork that can take place. What a Game Changer does is take all the competitors that are in a particular industry and allow for creativity and collaboration among them that fundamentally transforms the industry.

The Game Changer becomes the role model for everyone else who might have been their competitor. Their competitors see that the Game Changer has departed from the normal rules of competition and is doing something completely different. And instead of trying to compete with them, they want to learn from them.

Technological innovation based on "D.O.S."

Game Changers are increasingly possible in the 21st century because individual entrepreneurs can now have a personal, custom-designed working relationship with technology—and so can their existing and new customers:

1. Human-technology partnerships. More and more, entrepreneurs will create partnerships with technology, first of all for themselves and then for others by creating packaged human-technology partnerships. Each of these human-technology partnerships has the potential to be a Game Changer in a particular industry.

2. Dangers, Opportunities, Strengths. In Strategic Coach, we have a formula for discovering the specific present and future needs of any individual entrepreneur and customer: It's called D.O.S., which stands for Dangers, Opportunities, and Strengths. If you can zero in on the dangers your customers want eliminated, opportunities they want captured, and strengths they want maximized, you can create an automated service platform that meets their needs.

3. Automated teamwork platforms. More and more, providers of services are catering to the specific requirements of individuals. Therefore, if you can create an interface between what D.O.S. the customer has on their mind and your ability to respond to that in an alert, curious, responsive, and resourceful way, you completely bypass your competition.

Game changing from isolation to teamwork.

The chances today of people feeling left out, feeling left behind, feeling completely alone, feeling overwhelmed, or feeling bewildered goes up as the rate of change around them goes up. This means that your increasingly successful business consists of taking people in particular situations of isolation; custom-designing their particular needs for the future; building, first of all, human teamwork around them to permanently solve their particular set of isolation issues; and then automating the teamwork.

Your competition, realizing that they're being bypassed, are willing to become your students and customers to understand this new game—because the opportunity in the new game is exponentially bigger. That's a future prospect that is worth mastering with your Ambition Scorecard.

Mindset 8:
The Exponential Neighborhood

Of all the mindsets we've covered in the Ambition Scorecard, this eighth and final one may be what challenges you the most because it involves choosing who gets to come along with you into your bigger and better future.

Who are you hanging out with right now and as you go forward? Are they future-focused people who are continually creating a future that's bigger than their past?

If your answer is yes, then you are already living in what I call an Exponential Neighborhood. When I say "exponential," I'm referring to growth that multiplies itself and is closely associated in the 21st century with an accelerating rate of technological change.

And though "neighborhood" ordinarily means a physical place, in this context it means an entrepreneurial network of like-minded individuals who are taking advantage of exponential technology in building their bigger and better futures.

Living in an Exponential Neighborhood, then, means continually surrounding yourself with ambition entrepreneurs who are focused on and excited about growth.

Who you hang out with makes a big difference.

We're positively and negatively influenced by the people in our lives, so it's important for your confidence to be surrounded by the right people. And if you want to create a Self-Multiplying Company, it's necessary to be around people for whom multiplying is the normal way of going about things.

Exponential, again, simply means growth that grows itself: two times two is four, and four times four is 16, and 16

21ST CENTURY BREAKTHROUGH
EVERYONE EXCITED ABOUT GROWTH
GROWTH!
GROWTH!
GROWTH!
AMBITION SCORECARD
GROWTH!
GROWTH!
GROWTH!
GROWTH!
EVERYTHING'S HEADING THIS WAY
1950
TODAY
I.P.O.
Kid Genius Invents TV App, Becomes Newest Tech Millionaire

times 16 is 256, and so forth. Exponential growth like this was possible in limited ways the industrial age of the 20th century, but now that we're in the microchip age, thinking about your future growth in exponential ways makes the greatest entrepreneurial sense.

In order for you to think this way, it's necessary to surround yourself with other people who also think this way. That's your Exponential Neighborhood.

In 1950, when I was six years old, I had a big goal that my family would get a television set. Today, there are six-year-olds whose big goal is to create a mobile app that deserves to have an IPO on Wall Street. Six-year-olds today have "exponential" built into their thinking because they've never lived in a world that operated any other way.

Over the next 25 years, the more you surround your personal entrepreneurial ambition with exponentially-minded achievers, the faster your bigger and better progress will start to multiply itself.

Growing exponentially, both inside and out.

A famous motivational speaker by the name of Charlie "Tremendous" Jones was quoted as saying, "You will be the same person in five years as you are today except for the people you meet and the books you read." The people in your life change you, and it's important to be surrounded by individuals who are excited about the possibilities of exponential growth in their personal life, in their entrepreneurial life, in their teamwork within their organizations, and in their teamwork with other entrepreneurs.

Mindset 6 was about creating your Self-Multiplying Company. In order for that to happen in an accelerating fashion, you as the owner-entrepreneur have to be completely comfortable with, and enthusiastic about, exponential capabilities, resources, and opportunities.

You're the key: If you're comfortable with growth multiplying growth in your own life, then everybody in your company will take their cues from your exponential mindset. Everybody on your team will want to be part of your personally expanding Exponential Neighborhood.

It's like living in a neighborhood where everyone is upwardly mobile in an exponential way. In some cases, this actually happens physically—people will live in a physical neighborhood or part of a city that is more directed toward an exponential future than others. But with global communications now, you can do this electronically, and it's easier than ever to meet and work with other exponentially-minded people.

Your other mindsets make this eighth one easy.

It's very difficult for most people and many entrepreneurs to think in exponential terms because they don't have anyone else in their daily life thinking this way. But your entrepreneurial ambition over many years has brought you to the point where living and working in an Exponential Neighborhood is your next logical step.

People in an Exponential Neighborhood have an advanced sense of personal ambition that corresponds to the eight mindsets on the Ambition Scorecard.

The Exponential Neighborhood is your eighth ambition mindset because each one of the previous seven mindsets is a necessary foundational support for exponential thinking.

Let's do a quick review to see how this works: You're coming from a mindset of "wanting" rather than needing. You're thinking in terms of 25 years rather than short term, which means you have all the time in the world to achieve many 10x breakthroughs. You can continually achieve these breakthroughs through your five 90-day Moving Future Multipliers.

You're living a life where every 90-day jump in personal and organizational achievement makes up just one percent of the 100 quarters you've given yourself for your ambition. All along the way, you feel increasingly clear and simple

because every achievement is structured within a 4 C's Formula of increasing commitment, courage, capability, and confidence. Because of this, your personal freedoms of Time, Money, Relationship, and Purpose naturally take the organizational form of a Self-Multiplying Company, which as it grows, automatically becomes a Game Changer in your marketplace and industry.

As you follow the strengthening power of the other seven mindsets, you can see that not only is living for the rest of your personal and work life in an Exponential Neighborhood a desirable possibility, it's actually the only possibility. Being "exponential" will happen automatically for you, and having made this jump for yourself, you'll automatically begin helping more and more people do it for themselves.

Conclusion:
Scoring Expands Your Ambition

In 1890, William James, one of America's greatest philosophers wrote:

"The greatest discovery of my generation is that a human can alter his life by altering his attitudes of mind."

Mindset now becomes the central tool for personal empowerment, transformation, and ambition. And where people have gotten very used to measuring external progress, there's now something that's more fundamentally important, which is that *we can now measure the mindsets that led to the external performance and results.*

Complete methodology: With the Ambition Scorecard, we've developed a complete methodology for identifying the mindsets that make up the best entrepreneurial ambition, and we found a way for you to identify exactly where you fall on a scorecard of contrasting attitudes.

You are able then to give a score to each mindset and give yourself a total score that represents your current level of ambition.

Once you have your current score, you can compare where you are today with where you were in the past at various intervals. You can also measure your mindsets against the mindsets of people you live with and the society you came out of. As a result, you're able to make decisions, communicate, plan, and take actions that are in alignment with the higher-level mindsets and thereby improve. You're able to grow your mindset through the Scorecard.

SCORING YOUR PROGRESS
90 DAYS
90 DAYS
60
72
83
92
AMBITION
EVERYONE WILL NOTICE

Everyone around you will notice the shift.

If you adapt these eight mindsets—which have been tested and experimented with for over 30 years with thousands of entrepreneurs—and continually make them the basis for your self-improvement, planning, and organizational improvement, your creative and transformative ambition will continually grow.

In the 10x Ambition Program, we review the Scorecard every quarter, and participants discuss it at each workshop. I recommend reviewing your own Scorecard every 90 days and creating a game plan of decisions, communications, and actions that will raise your scores in each of the areas. When you make an improvement in your overall mindset, you'll notice it.

Discovering your neighborhood: Those around you will notice it as well, and you'll begin attracting into your life people who either consciously or unconsciously are also high on the Scorecard. It's your number-one way of discovering who makes up your community and who belongs in your Exponential Neighborhood.

Custom-designed to your unique ambitions.

Over thousands of years, humans have created an incomparable array of tools for measuring and scoring. We love scoring. Humans can't make progress unless they have the ability to measure performance and results over time. This is especially true for those who are ambition entrepreneurs.

Measuring and scoring entrepreneurial mindsets is the very essence of human development on a personal level, group level, society level, and civilization level.

The most successful entrepreneurs on the planet are the best scorers. They're the best measurers. They're the ones with the best scoring systems. The ones with the biggest ambitions.

With the Ambition Scorecard, we're taking all of the previous measurement progress around the world and raising it to the level of those crucial mindsets that support the greatest entrepreneurial achievement.

Everything in the Ambition Scorecard is custom-designed to your specific ambitions in life. Although all ambition entrepreneurs have these eight common mindset measurements, you will interpret them uniquely in terms of your own experience and your own Unique Ability.

The Strategic Coach Program

Your Lifetime Entrepreneurial Ambition

The Strategic Coach Program, by its very nature, has qualifications and measurements that attract a particular type of talented, successful, and ambitious entrepreneur. One differentiating quality of these Strategic Coach participants is that they recognize that the technology-empowered 21st century is a unique time to be an entrepreneur. They accept that if they can focus on mastering the right mindsets, they can experience breakthroughs for themselves, both personally and professionally, that are new in history.

It's the first time that entrepreneurial individuals with no special birth privileges and no special education can achieve almost anything they set their minds to.

Mindsets that transform potential into reality.

Many entrepreneurs have the potential and the willingness to achieve exponential goals in the 21st century, but they are blocked from taking action and making progress because they feel trapped in three ways:

- **Trapped thinking:** They are isolated by their own disconnected creativity, which continually churns out new ideas that don't translate into achievement.

- **Trapped circumstances:** They are surrounded by people who don't support their ambitions, who actively oppose them, or who try to make them feel guilty about their achievements and dreams.

- **Trapped energy:** They're using much of their daily energy to simply sustain themselves without ever actually experiencing exponential performance and results.

HISTORIC BREAKTHROUGH
2000
2100
ENTREPRENEURISM
TRAPPED!
SITUATIONS
PEOPLE
THOUGHTS
YOUR AMBITION
GAME CHANGER
10X AMBITION
FOUNDATION
STRATEGIC COACH

Around the world, the vast majority of entrepreneurs never get out of these trapped circumstances, but at Strategic Coach, we've taken a look at what goes on in the minds of the best entrepreneurs and have created a thinking system that is custom-designed for them and adjusts to the ambition of each individual.

The Strategic Coach Program provides an accelerating lifetime structure, process, and community for these entrepreneurs to create exponential breakthroughs.

Upward jumps of entrepreneurial ambition.

Depending on where you are right now in your life and business, we have a complete set of entrepreneurial mindsets that will immediately "jump" you up to the next level in terms of your ambition, achievements, and progress. Over the course of your entrepreneurial lifetime, you can move upward through our three levels of mindset measurement and scoring:

1. Foundation: From isolation to teamwork. At this first breakthrough level, you create a Unique Ability Team that allows you to have a Self-Managing Company.

2. 10x Ambition: From teamwork to exponential. You make breakthroughs that transform your life into an Exponential Neighborhood and your organization becomes a Self-Multiplying Company.

3. Game Changer: From exponential to transformative. As your entrepreneurial life becomes exponential, your Self-Multiplying Company become transformative. The key evidence of this is that your biggest competitors want to become your best students, customers, and promoters.

The question now is where your mindsets fall on the Ambition Scorecard. Your current score tells you in what areas of your life and business you'll want to improve so you can raise your overall levels of ambition the next time.

While you can work toward making these improvements on your own, it's much faster, simpler, and more enjoyable to make these transformative changes in a community of like-minded peers and through the ambition levels of Strategic Coach, which is designed to support your upward jumps for the rest of your life.

For more information about the Strategic Coach Program, visit us online at *strategiccoach.com* or call us at 416.531.7399 or 1.800.387.3206.

About The Author
Dan Sullivan

Dan Sullivan is the founder and president of The Strategic Coach Inc. and creator of the Strategic Coach® Program, which helps accomplished entrepreneurs reach new heights of success and happiness. He has over 40 years of experience as a strategic planner and coach to entrepreneurial individuals and groups. He is author of over 30 publications, including *The Great Crossover, The 21st Century Agent, Creative Destruction,* and *How The Best Get Better®*, and co-author of *The Laws of Lifetime Growth* and *The Advisor Century*.